AN ORDINARY POLISH BOY

JOURNEY TO ENGLAND
A TRIBUTE TO MY FATHER

BY BRENDAN REDKO

AN ORDINARY POLISH BOY: JOURNEY TO ENGLAND

My father's 'Journey to England' starts in the small town of Tomaszow Lubelski in the Lublin / Lubelskie district of south east Poland. This map depicts the post war borders. The 1939 borders with Russia extended much further to the east and included the Ukrainian areas of Volhynia and Galicia.

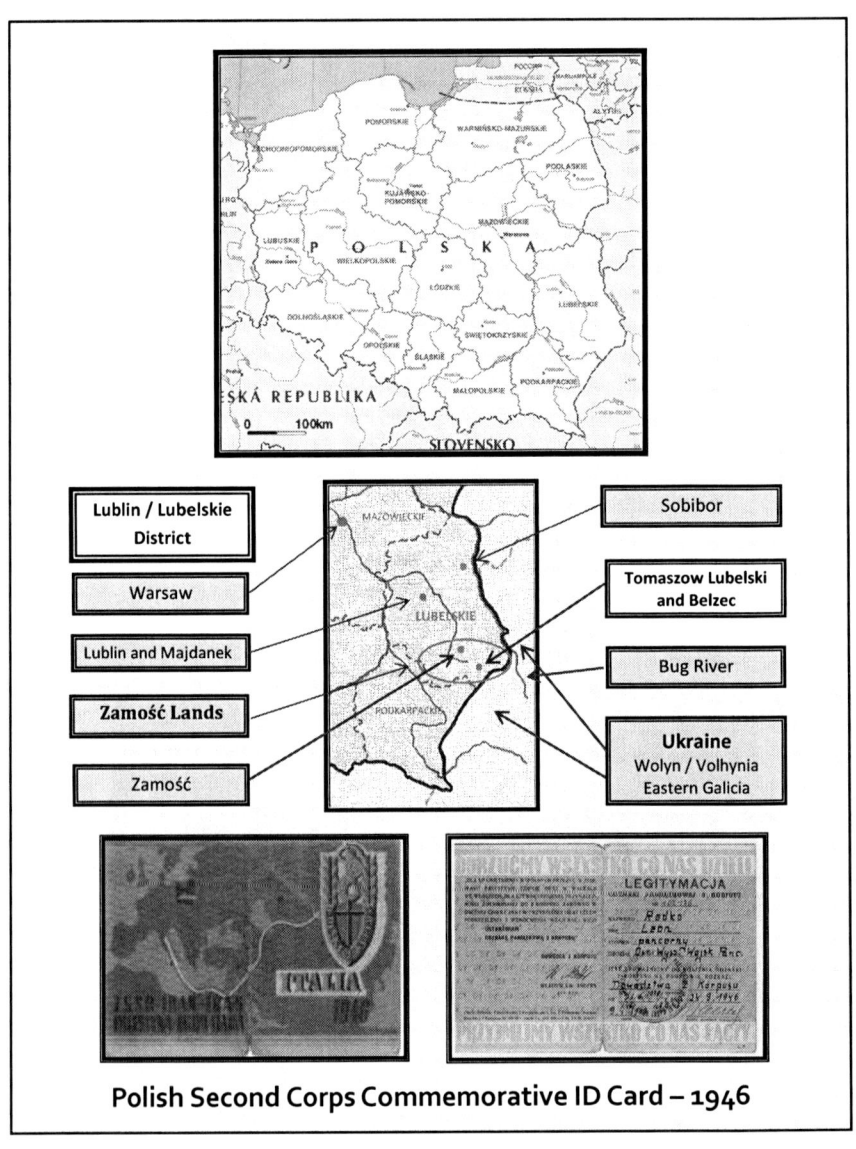

Polish Second Corps Commemorative ID Card – 1946

I dedicate this story to

A man I never really knew, a man I wish I had got to know:

My father,

Leon Redko (1925-1996)

An ordinary Polish boy who saw things that no one should have to see, who, with hundreds of thousands of other ordinary Polish people, saw his life devastated and changed forever by the brutality and violence of Hitler's and Stalin's wars.

To all the victims of the events in this story:

We need to remember—lest we forget!

AuthorHouse™
1663 Liberty Drive
Bloomington, IN 47403
www.authorhouse.com
Phone: 1-800-839-8640

© 2013 by Brendan Redko. All rights reserved.

No part of this book may be reproduced, stored in a retrieval system, or transmitted by any means without the written permission of the author.

Published by AuthorHouse   04/05/2013

ISBN: 978-1-4817-8234-0 (sc)
ISBN: 978-1-4817-8235-7 (e)

Any people depicted in stock imagery provided by Thinkstock are models, and such images are being used for illustrative purposes only.
Certain stock imagery © Thinkstock.

This book is printed on acid-free paper.

Because of the dynamic nature of the Internet, any web addresses or links contained in this book may have changed since publication and may no longer be valid. The views expressed in this work are solely those of the author and do not necessarily reflect the views of the publisher, and the publisher hereby disclaims any responsibility for them.

Introduction

In 2011 a Polish work colleague asked me about my surname. I told her that my father was Polish and that he had come to England after the Second World War as a refugee. She then asked me if I would be willing to give an interview describing how he came to be in England on the radio show *Radiowski*, a weekly programme produced by the Polish community in Bristol.

I soon realised that, although I knew that my father had come from a town called Tomaszow Lubelski and that he had been taken into forced labour, I actually knew very little about him and even less about Poland, its history, or what happened during the war. I declined my colleague's offer, as I did not think I had any real story to tell.

Just before Christmas 2011, however, I found all my father's old documents in the attic and, remembering my colleague's offer, I thought I might try to find out more. I then used Google Translate and online history archives to build a timeline of what was happening in the locations he was in at the various stages of his life, as indicated by his photos and papers.

As my investigation continued, I found myself wanting to find out more about my Polish roots and what the Polish people faced at the hands of the Germans. From my point of view, although I knew about the Holocaust, I actually knew very few details, so my story also became a sort of introduction to these events as I discovered the magnitude and brutality of the occupation, not just where my father lived but also throughout Eastern Europe, in particular in Russia, Ukraine and the Baltic states.

My book describes what happened in his home town and in eastern Poland after the Germans invaded and how my father eventually came to England after the war. I named the story *An Ordinary Polish Boy* because it became evident from my research that my father's story was the same as those of tens of thousands of other ordinary Polish people caught up in the horror and turmoil of the times. I wanted my book, in some way, to remember my father's story as well as what all these other ordinary people faced and how they struggled to survive and to hopefully ensure that these events are never forgotten. In the end, I was so moved by what I found out that I decided to do the radio interview.

I would like to give a special mention and thank-you to Basia Augustyniak Everett from Krakow, my Polish work colleague whose original question encouraged me to research my Polish roots and to Magda Bond from Rzeszów/ Podkarpacie, who as producer of the show *Radiowski* on Bristol Community Fm Radio organised the interview. It was through their continued interest and support that convinced me that this was a story that should be told and remembered.

An Ordinary Polish Boy: Journey to England

As I retrieved the Christmas decorations from the attic, I came across an old small suitcase which held a few fading photos and documents that had belonged to my father, who had died in 1996. They brought back a lot of memories. I knew little about my father. As a child, I hardly saw him; he worked fourteen hours a day, seven days a week as a welder and mechanic. I knew he was Polish and that he had been fourteen when the Second World War started. I also knew he had been taken into forced labour by the Germans and that he was never able to return to his family after the war, but apart from that, I knew little else.

So at the age of fifty-seven, I decided to try to find out what happened. I cannot remember having one conversation with my father when I was a child. He was not someone who enjoyed conversation, and he never really spoke about his early life, but I did remember a few sentences he had said about incidents in the war. These few sentences were usually made as quick comments with no further explanation in response to events in various films we had watched on television. It was these few sentences, along with the documents and photos that I discovered in the attic, that enabled me to piece together a short history of my father's life and times.

As I started to build the timeline of his life, I was drawn into a story I wanted to investigate further: a story of betrayal of countries, broken promises and horrors impossible to comprehend.

My father was born on 6 August 1925 in Tomaszow Lubelski, a small town of about 12,000 inhabitants in the Voivodeship of Lublin in south-east Poland.

The area was still recovering from the aftermath of the 1921 Polish-Russian war and the First World War. It had been the site of major battles in both conflicts with German, Austrian and Ukrainian forces taking turns to control the region. Warfare and destruction continued through the 1920s, with Ukrainian paramilitary soldiers raiding the town, looting, raping and murdering local people.

Left: My father, 1940 at back on the right. His father to his left and brothers in front.

Right: His mother and family members.

Times were hard—families eked out a living from the land and from occasional labouring and factory work. The average farming family occupied a one-room dwelling, usually without a toilet or running water, and often without electricity or gas. These tiny dwellings were often occupied by five or more people who ate what they could grow or produce they had bought at the local market.

The population of Tomaszow was evenly split between about six thousand Jews and an equal number of Christians. My father's family was Roman Catholic. Anti-Semitism and tensions between Jews and non-Jews were often high; according to my father, the Jews seemed to have most of the jobs and businesses and therefore more money than the non-Jewish residents. This occasionally sparked conflict, with anti-Semite groups holding meetings and attacking Jewish businesses in the town, but on the whole, everyone just got on with their lives and supported their families the best they could.

My father told me how, as a child, he worked at night in a bakery and was paid in bread. Life was a struggle, particularly through the Depression and the economic difficulties which lasted from 1926 to 1936. Many survived only with the aid of soup kitchens organised by community leaders. Local people looked to emigrate if they could to escape poverty.

Left: An unpaved road in Tomaszow Lubelski, 1939. Right: A market in Tomaszow, 1938.
(Photo sources 1 and 2)

As 1939 approached, my father was living on the outskirts of Tomaszow with his parents, two much older brothers and a sister. His father, a man in his fifties with a full head of silver hair, worked the land as a peasant farmer to provide for his family. My father was very close to his mother, who doted on him, as he was the baby of the family. He told me once that his mother said he could run so fast, his heels would touch his backside as he played with friends in the fields surrounding his home. He also told me that although everyone was poor, families always worked hard together to provide the basic necessities for survival, like food and clothes.

However, everything was set to change!

On 1 September 1939, when my father was just fourteen, Germany launched its invasion of Poland, with 1.8 million soldiers using the *blitzkrieg* method of total war. As they advanced, they bombed whole towns and cities and the people in them. The Polish Army fought strongly, but they had no chance.

Although Poland and Russia had signed a non-aggression pact to ensure peace between the two countries, Hitler also had a secret agreement with Russia and Stalin to partition Poland, which would enable Russia to annex about half of the Polish state. Thousands of Russian soldiers also invaded from the east to support this plan.

Although news of the German invasion had reached Tomaszow, my father told me that no one really expected it to affect them. People just carried on with their day-to-day lives. On Wednesday, 6 September, however, German planes burst out of the skies dropping bombs on homes in an attempt to destroy much of the town. There were no military targets in the area—ordinary people were the targets. A massive fire developed in the Jewish sector of town, destroying many homes and the synagogue. Well over a hundred people were killed.

Left: German soldiers marching into Poland. Right: German planes bombing a Polish city.
(Photo sources 3 and 4)

I remember my father commenting on how frightening it was to be in an air raid, with explosions getting closer and closer. Everyone was in a state of shock and didn't know what to do because they had not expected anything like this to happen. When the attack had finished and people came out of their homes, my father saw that much of the town had been flattened, numerous fires were burning, and people were lying dead and injured in the streets.

After the Battles of Tomaszow Lubelski, 17-26 September 1939

Left: Russian and German officers plan the battle. Middle: Scenes from the battle. Right: Tomaszow children in the ruins. (Photo sources 5, 6 and 7)

Left: Tomaszow after the battle. Right: Scenes from the battle just outside the town. (Photo sources 8 and 9)

Left: Polish Vickers tanks captured at the battle. Right: More ruins from outside Tomaszow (Photo sources 10 and 11)

German Army units then entered Tomaszow on 13 September chasing small Polish Army groups still trying to defend their country. By this time, the Polish Army, struggling to hold the Germans in other parts of the country, was ordered to retreat to the Tomaszow and Zamość region in the south-east of the country to regroup and organise themselves to make a stand against the invaders.

The Polish Army, now numbering over two hundred thousand, tried to set up defensive positions but had become squeezed by several hundred thousand German soldiers and tanks attacking from the west and thousands of Russians advancing from the east. The Poles, however, were confident they could hold the enemy; they had signed treaties with powerful Allies in the West.

They were now waiting for Britain and France to support them as they should have done under the terms of the Common Defence Pact which had been signed in August 1939 and guaranteed military intervention in the event of an invasion.

Although Britain and France had both declared war on Germany on 3 September as a response to the invasion they provided no support to Poland.

The Russian Army had invaded Poland from the east under the pretext of providing support for minority ethnic groups in the area. Although they had made an agreement to support the Germans, they were not actually involved in the fighting yet. They were, at this time, wary of taking on France and Britain, but as soon as it became obvious that the French and British were not going to provide any military support to Poland, the Russians also attacked the Poles.

On 17 September, the first battle of Tomaszow Lubelski started. It became the second biggest battle of the war in Poland, with nearly a million men, including large numbers of infantry, tanks and cavalry units from the three armies engaged in fighting over a wide area. The battle also spread into the town, and as the fighting increased in intensity, local people also became caught up in the mayhem. Many died as homes and buildings were destroyed.

The Germans then took control of the town for a few days, brutalising local inhabitants, particularly the Jews, before they withdrew on 20 September, leaving the Russians in control. Polish reinforcements arrived in the area on 22 September to support the remnants of the Polish Army struggling to defend their country, and the second battle of Tomaszow Lubelski started.

As this battle got underway, the Polish Army saw some success when General Anders and his cavalry managed to break through German lines on the first day, but elsewhere, the Army's defences were struggling to hold the Germans. The battle continued until 26 September when, overwhelmed by superior numbers, the Polish Army finally capitulated to the German and Russian forces and either surrendered or retreated.

Polish cavalry could not cope with the mechanised German forces. (Photo source 12 and 13)

On 27 September 1939, the Russian Army withdrew to the agreed partition line along the Bug River, a few miles east of Tomaszow, and left the area to the Germans. Many Poles were captured, although about a hundred thousand managed to escape to Romania, where they organised the Polish Army of the East and continued the war with great effect through Asia, Africa and Europe until Germany surrendered in 1945.

My father commented on how terrifying the total war was as it played out in and around Tomaszow. Much of the battle was fought in a series of skirmishes over a large area, and as the Polish Army retreated, they left dead and injured soldiers and hundreds of horses where they fell. He told me that it became normal to see dead bodies every day; everyone just got used to the sight.

I now also understood his often repeated dislike of the Russians, whose cruelty and ruthlessness he felt was worse than that of the Germans. He told me that he was actually more frightened of them than the Germans. During the battle, the Russians captured thousands of Polish soldiers, executing anyone who resisted and shooting many of the officers as soon as they were captured. They also executed forty-two patients and staff in a Polish military hospital near Zamość during the battle and then executed a Polish General after he was captured and interrogated.

By the end of September 1939, the Germans had secured Tomaszow and the surrounding countryside. The Germans' superior weaponry was decisive in containing the area and the local population. The bravery of Polish Army and its cavalry units had been ineffective against the more mechanised German Army, and thousands were killed or captured. The Germans then organised the whole region as a separate administrative region of the Third Reich calling it the General Government, the area included much of central and southern Poland.

The Russians had withdrawn their forces back to their homeland, which now included all the newly annexed parts of eastern Poland, which amounted to about half of the original Polish state and included 13 million inhabitants. As they withdrew, they also took over a million Polish prisoners with them, including over two hundred thousand captured soldiers and thousands of educated Poles from the occupied land in an attempt to remove Polish influence from these areas.

Many of these prisoners were taken to concentration camps in Russia and Siberia, where a large number died as a result of the conditions. The Polish Institute of National Remembrance estimated that at least a hundred and fifty thousand Poles were killed as Russia took control of its newly annexed lands.

Many of the captured Polish officers were taken to execution sites, where the Russians carried out one of the most infamous acts of the war. After Stalin's order on 5 March 1940, thousands of Polish officers were taken to pits dug in the Katyn forest in Russia and, in small groups, shot in the back of the head before being pushed into the pits on top of their already dead colleagues.

These executions, carried out in secret during April and May 1940, were intended to deprive Poland of potential leaders capable of organising any form of resistance in the newly annexed lands.

Twenty-one thousand officers, police and educated Poles were killed by the Russians during these atrocities, and tens of thousands more are still unaccounted for. When the Germans found the graves in 1943, the Russians accused the Germans of committing the atrocity. The Allies accepted this, as it was more important that they maintain their alliance with Russia in the fight against Germany rather than to find out the truth.

Left: Polish officers captured by the Russians—their fate likely to be at Katyn.
Right: German propaganda poster blaming the Russians for the atrocity.
(Photo sources 14 and 15)

With the Polish defeat at Tomaszow, the Germans were now in total control of the country, and as the occupation continued, they put into place their plans for the population. Throughout Poland, the Germans enforced new decrees particularly relating to the treatment of the Jews. These decrees were intended to dehumanise the population. These included curfews and a variety of other restrictions banning them from working, driving, buying medicine, using radios or telephones and taking large sums of money out of the bank.

In Tomaszow, about fifty Jewish families who had experienced the brutality of the Germans in the first occupation of the town decided to leave with the Russians when they withdrew on 27 September. The Jews who had chosen to stay behind were immediately subjected to beatings in the street and restrictions on where they could go, including a prohibition on using the main roads. Synagogues were closed and Jews were banned from practising their religion or attending prayer meetings.

The SS also evicted Jews from their homes as well as looting and burning their shops and businesses. A Jewish butcher had his fingers cut off so he could not slaughter animals according to kosher law.

Under penalty of death, Poles were forbidden to sell food to the Jews, many of whom were close to starvation. Jewish doctors were prevented from practising their skills, so with no doctors, medicine or food; malnutrition, disease and death became common, particularly among the very young and the old.

Left: Hitler Youth performing outside Tomaszow town hall, 1941.
The flags display the ancient Germanic sig, the rune symbol of victory.
Right: German soldiers rounding up people for slave labour after the battle of Tomaszow.
(Photo sources 16 and 17)

Groups of disabled Jews were forced into cellars, which were then filled with water until all inside drowned. The elderly and sick were routinely shot. One Jewish father was forced to choose which of his sons would be hanged. After saving one son, the father then committed suicide. People being hanged in the street became a common sight.

By April 1940, the Germans began building a forced labour camp at Belzec, a small village about three miles from Tomaszow. Jews, Polish tradesmen and Polish farm-worker prisoners were rounded up to build the camp. By November 1940, a Jewish ghetto in Tomaszow was established in the old market area. All the Jews in the town along with refugees from neighbouring villages and farms were forced to live in the ghetto.

Left: A Jewish work detail at Belzec labour camp. Right: Jewish forced labourers being marched to work. (Photo sources 18 and 19)

By December 1940, about six thousand Jews lived in the ghetto. The Germans also forced them to build camps for the occupying troops. In the early days of the occupation, partisans and Jews who had escaped the round-ups by hiding in the forests sabotaged some of the German plans. Tomaszow became an area of strong resistance, but reprisals were a constant threat to local people. Several German soldiers were killed by partisan actions in the town, which included an incident in which a grenade was thrown into the house where the soldiers were staying.

My father would become agitated as he recalled the fear that he and other local children felt about what the Resistance was doing at the beginning of the war, as the consequences for these actions were extreme. The Germans destroyed hundreds of villages throughout Poland, burning homes and executing thousands of inhabitants for resisting them or as a reprisal for partisan actions.

One German death would often lead to fifty Poles randomly selected and shot. He believed that with the Germans in such total control, much of this resistance at this time was futile and too dangerous. In some larger cities, up to thirty hostages were kept ready to be hanged in public every time there was a German death.

At the beginning of the occupation he felt that he was not actually in immediate danger as being a young farm boy he was not being targeted. As the number of executions throughout the area increased as a response to any partisan action, he said that local people were living in continual fear that they might be shot at any time.

As the occupation continued, a number of educated Poles and Jews were taken into the forests outside of Tomaszow, made to dig their own graves and shot. Surviving Jews held in the ghetto were made to wear an arm band with a yellow star on their jackets to indicate they were Jews. The ghetto was designed to contain the Jews so they would be ready for transportation to labour or extermination camps.

Despite the German agreement with Russia, which enabled the partition of Poland and the fact that they were allies together in the actual invasion, the overall German plan intended to also attack and invade Russia. This planned invasion of the Russian territories was intended to provide along with the Polish territory already captured the increased living space they wanted and to enable them to deal with the large Jewish communities living in Russia.

As the Germans prepared for war with Russia, their demand for workers increased. Poles over the age of fourteen were now registered for forced labour. The Polish forced labourers, unlike the Jews, were allowed to live in their homes.

**This is what happened to my father as
a fourteen-year-old boy**

By January 1940, the food supply was completely controlled by the Germans. Poles had to be registered for work to qualify for subsistence-level food rations and medicine. Some families tried to hide their children, but the risk of execution or removal to concentration camps was high, so nearly every one registered.

By early 1940, about thirty thousand Jews and a few hundred Gypsies from the area had been imprisoned at the labour camp at Belzec. They were forced to dig massive anti-tank trenches, the 'Otto Line' fortifications, on Poland's new eastern border in preparation for the German invasion of Russia in June 1941.

Thirty-five other forced-labour camps were established along the Otto Line under the control of the Belzec camp. Workers repaired and strengthened roads, regulated the flow of rivers and made other preparations for war with Russia.

Left: A woman about to be executed in Belzec camp. The soldier on left is a SS guard; the soldiers in the background are Ukrainian guards. Right: Executed prisoner on a latrine at Belzec. Both pictures were found on an SS soldier after he was captured. (Photo sources 20 and 21)

Conditions in the Belzec labour camps were appalling; prisoners were tortured, beaten and starved. Mothers killed their own babies because they didn't have enough food. SS guards killed people for fun and target practice. Prisoners were not allowed to use the latrines during the day, and anyone who tried to use them would be executed while sitting on the latrine.

These camps operated until early 1941. At least three hundred local people died in these camps in a few months. Twenty to thirty more who had become ill were sent back to the ghetto in Tomaszow every day to die, as with no medical aid, life expectancy was very short.

My father was registered for forced labour and groups of Polish farm worker prisoners from the Tomaszow area were also put to work in this area so it was possible that my father was working in the area before the Germans put the 'Operation Reinhard' plan into practice on the 17 March 1942.

This plan was also known as 'the Final Solution' and was agreed at a secret meeting at Wannsee on 20 January 1942 when the German leaders finalised how they would deal with the Jewish question.

Belzec was to become the first permanent extermination camp in the occupied territories. Unlike the hundreds of concentration camps, this camp was intended solely for killing and not for imprisonment. The camp was going to be used to experiment and refine the best ways to kill and dispose of thousands of people as soon as they arrived.

The Germans chose this location because the network of rail lines in the area made for easy transportation to the site from the large Jewish communities of south-east Poland.

The first round-up in Tomaszow of Jews destined for Belzec happened in March 1942. Jews were ordered to meet in the main square, having been told they were going to a work camp. As the round-up continued, a Jewish leader refused a request for the names of the Jews in town. He, his wife and his son were shot.

My father recalled seeing the Jews being rounded up in the town and then loaded onto lorries for the short ride to Belzec. Rumours of what was going to happen to these people spread, but few townspeople believed them. My father initially thought that most people in Tomaszow believed the Germans' story, that the Jews were going to be resettled in work camps in the East. He told me he later suspected that they were going to be killed, but at the time no one really knew.

Left: Jewish families Right: Gypsies before they were gassed at Belzec.
(Photo sources 22 and 23)

In the first two weeks of operation, sixty three thousand people were murdered at Belzec. This level of operation continued for another ten months. The truth of what was happening seemed too impossible to believe. When eyewitnesses gave accounts in London, the Allied governments also refused to believe the stories and did nothing to find out more or to help in any way.

What was happening, however, started to become common knowledge in Tomaszow by the end of 1942, when the reality of the earlier rumours were confirmed by Belzec villagers, who reported seeing thousands of people arriving at the station and going into the camp but no one ever leaving.

During the round-ups, the German SS troops and Gestapo surrounded whole areas and moved from house to house to ensure all the Jews had been taken to the square. Anyone—man, woman and child—not complying with orders or found hiding would be shot immediately.

Two more round-ups occurred in May and October 1942, and all the remaining Jews in Tomaszow were transported to Belzec. Anyone who showed defiance or who tried to run away was shot in the street. Maybe this relates to a comment my father made as we watched the film *Bullitt* when I was a child. He exclaimed after someone was shot in the film that the film was rubbish. He said, 'People don't fall like that when they are shot; it's not true!'

My father recalled his mother having to produce papers to show that he was Polish and not Jewish when he was rounded up at this time with Jewish children. The Germans let him go, but they took the others to the old market square to be loaded onto the lorries for the trip to Belzec where they all died.

My father also recalled German propaganda trying to divide the local Polish and Jewish populations by attempting to convince Polish people in Tomaszow that what was happening to the Jews was a good thing, claiming they were responsible for all the economic and social difficulties of the time. At least a thousand Poles from the wider region were also sent to be gassed at Belzec mainly for trying to help the Jews.

Left: Jewish families being forced onto cattle cars Right: More Jewish families arriving at Belzec. (Photo sources 24 and 25)

Belzec was to become the most efficient death camp of the war. The Germans used three wooden gas chambers before building six brick chambers. As systems improved, they could take two to three thousand men, women and children from arrival to cremation every two to three hours, killing up to fifteen thousand people a day.

Belzec's success paved the way for five more death camps in occupied Poland: Chelmno, Sobibor, Treblinka, Auschwitz and Majdanek. The systems developed and improved at Belzec were used as a model of good practice for the other camps. I now discovered that the Lublin district that my father had come from with its three death camps as well as the concentration camps, labour camps and mass execution sites had become the largest graveyard of murdered people the world had ever seen.

The United States Holocaust Memorial Museum estimate that between eleven and fifteen million people, including one million children and six million Jews, died in these six death camps and the concentration camps in Germany and Poland.

These death camps were intended to provide more efficient, cheaper and less stressful killing methods for the SS units, who had previously been responsible for carrying out all the mass executions since the invasion started.

The *Einsatzgruppen*, or SS Mobile Death Units, were the specialised German forces that entered Poland and continued into Russia, Ukraine and the Baltic states following the invasion under the pretext of containing guerrilla and local Partisan activity. They executed more than 1.5 million men, women and children; many women were raped before being shot.

The Mobile SS Death Units were also responsible for killing tens of thousands of educated Poles as part of Operation Tannenberg with twenty thousand Polish victims in over seven hundred mass executions in the first two months of the war. Operation Tannenberg was the plan implemented immediately after the invasion and was designed to eliminate the Polish political, religious and professional class and leave the country short of leaders.

The SS Mobile Death Units were also active in the Tomaszow area. Wajsleder Chana-Szpizajren, a Polish Jew from Tomaszow Lubelski, details an incident in her testimony written in 1949 in which a large number of Jewish farming families were rounded up and taken to

Tomaszow and then to the forest outside the town, where they were forced to dig their own graves before they were shot. Anyone trying to escape was immediately shot and killed.

Left: Young Jewish mother and her two children with a large group of Jews waiting to be executed at Lubny, Ukraine, on 16 October 1941. Right: Nazi soldier shooting a mother and child in 1942, at Ivangorod, Ukraine. (Photo sources 26 and 27)

As the Germans advanced further into Russia, Ukraine and the Baltic States, the Mobile Death Units were responsible for some of the most brutal atrocities of the war. They rounded up and shot Jews, Slavs, Communists and partisans by the thousands.

The SS units would order whole Jewish communities to meet at designated places for 'resettlement in the east'. Families would arrive with food and valuables for the journey. As they were marched to their destination, mothers would sing to their children to settle them, totally unaware of what was waiting for them. When they arrived at ravines or prepared pits, families were then separated and individuals were made to strip naked and then marched in small groups to the execution sites and shot.

Archive photos taken by the SS soldiers of naked women holding their babies and young children as they waited in line to be shot *only because they were Jewish* provide images beyond comprehension. The photos of naked children crying and mothers begging for their lives to no avail inspire incredulity and anger that humans can do what they did—but it happened.

Left: Young girls waiting to be executed at Babi Yar, Ukraine. Right: Jews being shot at Babi Yar. (Photo sources 28 and 29)

Rivka Yosilevska, a Polish Jew interviewed in the *World at War* television series in 1974, recalled standing in line, holding her young daughter as the families in front of her were led naked to the pit and shot. Her daughter pleaded, 'Mommy, they are killing us. Why don't we run away?' Rivka could only answer, 'Where shall we run?' before they were both led to the pit and shot. The daughter died, but the mother survived, waking up later, lying in the pit along with five hundred bodies.

The *Einsatzgruppen* were also responsible for the most infamous massacre of the war at Babi Yar in the Ukraine. The soldiers rounded up 33,771 Jewish men, women and children from Kiev and marched them to the Babi Yar ravine, where they were shot in an action that lasted two days on 29 and 30 September 1941.

No words can express the cruelty and barbarism of the German invaders!

With Belzec fully operational from March 1942, the transportation of Jews to the site continued almost daily apart from a short break in May when the brick gas chambers were built to improve efficiency.

My father must have lived or worked near the railway line at this time, as he told me that he used to see two or three trains a day going towards Belzec. These trains would be pulling up to fifty cattle cars per transport, with each car holding about one hundred people.

By then everyone knew what was going to happen to them, but no one could do anything about it, local people just accepted what was happening and were just thankful it wasn't happening to them.

Archived material from Belzec death camp makes for haunting reading. Lists and lists of whole families, mothers, fathers, sons, daughters, children, babies—all killed. Family portraits of those who died make it even harder to comprehend what happened. Typical family photographs like those we all have at home—smiling family groups in their best clothes, young girls in pigtails smiling, young boys looking serious.

No one could guess what was coming!

Left: Gate sign at the site of the death camp at Belzec. Right: Jewish families arriving by train to be exterminated. (Photo sources 30 and 31)

The victims, mainly Jews and some Gypsies would arrive at Belzec by lorry or train; as they stepped from the transport, victims underwent a 'selection': stronger males would be selected to live so they could work.

The rest would be separated from their partners and made to strip. Women had their hair shaved and were then forced to run naked with their children through a barbed-wire tunnel just two metres wide to the shower rooms while being whipped and bayoneted by shouting Ukrainian guards with dogs.

With most still believing that this was a transit camp and unaware of what was going to happen, they were forced into the shower rooms, except that the shower rooms concealed the newly invented method of mass extermination: the gas chamber. The victims were crammed tightly into the room—with up to eight hundred people occupying just twenty-five square metres of space—before the doors were locked and sealed with sand.

Carbon monoxide was then pumped in from diesel engines hidden outside. As these victims were being put to death, local people reported hearing the women screaming and wailing, children crying, dogs barking, men shouting and occasional gunfire—and then the silence.

As the horrors continued, the German camp orchestra would play its music, usually loud marching tunes, intended to hide the sounds of the exterminations. The guards would then look through the peepholes of the gas chambers to check that the gas had done its job. Then, those selected to live earlier now had their job to do: remove any gold teeth from the bodies with hammers and then drag the dead to the pits to be buried or cremated. Then, after the next selection, they also went to the gas chambers.

No vision of hell could compete with these scenes!

The diesel engines providing the carbon monoxide would often fail, leaving the victims waiting in the gas chambers for up to two hours before mechanics fixed them. The trains often delivered more than five thousand people at a time, but the gas chambers' capacity was between two and three thousand, so the rest had to wait locked in the cattle cars until it was there turn, sometimes overnight if they arrived late.

As the knowledge of what was happening spread, many of the prisoners held in the trains tried to escape, but the guards were efficient. No one escaped; anyone who attempted to run was either shot or bayoneted to death.

Left: Smiling Ukrainian guards and captured Red Army soldiers who volunteered their services, some just twenty years old, at Belzec. Right: SS officers stationed in Belzec. Just 20 SS officers and about 100 Ukrainian guards ran the complex. (Photo sources 32 and 33)

A pit was always ready at Belzec for defiant prisoners. As soon as they arrived at the selection area, they would be taken away, shot straight away and thrown into the pit. One group contained so many difficult prisoners that the guards ran out of ammunition. They completed these executions with a pickaxe handle.

In the first few months of experimenting with the best killing techniques, Captain Wirth, the Belzec camp commandant, decided to use carbon monoxide for the executions, as he felt that the amount of the insecticide Zyklon B needed might compromise the secrecy of what was happening as the number of deliveries to the camp would be so high that it would become obvious to too many people.

Continual problems with the diesel engines however, eventually led to the use of Zyklon B, which was a more efficient method of killing. All the guards had to do was drop the pellets into the chamber to produce the toxic cyanide gas and complete the killing process.

After the first few months of exterminations, the dead were buried in pits, but the bodies soon putrefied and expanded as they released gases, breaking up the soil and forcing the bodies to rise out of the ground.

Local people reported that the smell from the tens of thousands of bodies in the pits was unbearable. Other ways had to be found to dispose of them. Cremation was decided upon as the best way to deal with the massive piles of naked bodies that were building up.

The huge numbers of open-air cremations that were needed put so much human fat into the air that it stuck to windows and blocked out light in local people's homes. This thick, black human-ash-filled smoke from these cremations could be seen in Tomaszow and for miles through the surrounding area and ensured that what was happening at Belzec became common knowledge

There are very few stories from inmates of Belzec compared to inmates of other camps—only two inmates are known to have survived. One of the worst stories relates to the arrival of a consignment of children under three. They were all thrown screaming and crying into a pit and then buried alive. Chaim Hirszman, one of those two survivors commented that he could never forget how the earth continued to move until the children had all taken their last breaths.

By late 1942, the German leaders started to think about what they should do with the death camps. Some felt that Germany should be proud of sites such as Belzec and that they should be preserved as monuments to the courage and bravery of the soldiers entrusted with carrying out the 'Final Solution' and all the 'unpleasantness' that it involved!

In the end, particularly as the Allies were gaining control in the war, it was decided that other nations might not view the camps in the same way, so they decided to hide the evidence. To do this, they needed to exhume the bodies, cremate them and crush any remaining bones.

At Belzec, this meant digging up and burning up to four thousand bodies a day on four massive outdoor pyres. As this work was being carried out, new consignments of Jews continued to arrive to be gassed.

Left: Funeral pyre at Belzec camp. Right: Bone-crushing machine used to hide the evidence. (Photo sources 34 and 35)

This process continued from November 1942 to March 1943. Five hundred Jewish prisoners were selected to do the work. When they had completed the task, they were all taken to Sobibor to be gassed, although many were shot instead after they arrived because they guessed what was going to happen to them and tried to run away as soon as they got off the train.

The last memory before Belzec closed came from a German worker who recalled the young Jewish office girls who had been forced to keep the camp files and records being taken out and gassed in a portable gas-chamber van.

When Belzec camp stopped its killing operations in December 1942, nearly six hundred thousand people had been murdered there in the ten months it was in operation—an average rate of nearly two thousand people killed every day!

By early 1943, the camp was no longer needed. There weren't any Jews left in the area to kill, and bigger camps such as Auschwitz took over when the Germans started transporting people, mainly Jews, by the tens of thousands from other captured countries to be killed.

As the camp was decommissioned, the gas chambers were dismantled and the site grassed over to disguise it as farmland. The bone-crushing machine was taken to another death camp where the same evidence-hiding work was being carried out.

Left: Belzec gas chambers, covered by woodland, 2002. Right: Belzec Station. (Photo sources 36 and 37)

The Germans then gave the land to a Ukrainian guard and his family to farm. They also landscaped much of the area with fir trees and wild lupines to cover the mass graves. When the area was liberated by the Russians in 1944 there were few signs of what had happened there. A memorial sculpture was built in the 1960's which quickly became overgrown. A new larger memorial and museum was eventually built in 2003 and even today, visitors can still see 'white stones'—crushed bones and teeth—mixed in with the soil.

The German Nazi philosophy was that Jews, all Gypsies, Roma and Sinti, all Slavs including Poles and Russians, all people of colour, homosexuals and the physically or mentally disabled were subhuman and therefore should be systematically killed as part of the German plan to promote the purity of the Aryan master race.

A non-Aryan person only survived if they were of any value to Germany, for example, if they were fit enough to work. That person would be registered for work and forced to labour for the Germans. If the long hours and intensity of the work didn't kill them, the starvation diet, extreme cold, poor living conditions and disease in the labour camps were likely to. Non-Aryan workers were considered expendable and would be worked until they died.

My father used to comment on how extreme the winters could be in Poland, with the temperature sometimes dropping to minus 25 centigrade, with no heating in either working or living conditions, the cold became unbearable. Even without heating or adequate clothing, he said that you just got used to the cold because you had to.

As the war developed into a global conflict, with the fighting spreading to North Africa and Scandinavia as well as the Eastern and Western Fronts, Germany was becoming desperate for workers to maintain the war effort. They needed labour to produce food and provisions for the German military and for the civilians back home. A huge amount of labour was also required to maintain output in the factories and for construction.

Albert Speer, as the German Minister for Armaments and War Production, was responsible for deploying this forced labour. It was his request for labour to maintain the war effort which gave rise to the forced labour programme. For this role, he was found guilty of crimes against humanity after the war and imprisoned for twenty years at Nuremburg.

The Army and its supply network also needed additional manpower to make up for the losses already suffered. By the end of 1943, twelve million workers, nearly two million from Poland alone, had been forcibly taken from the captured countries and transported to Berlin.

As part of the plan to meet this need, an order went out from Berlin in November 1942 for the SS to collect one hundred and ten thousand able-bodied young Poles from three hundred towns and villages from the Lublin district of occupied Poland and take them back to Berlin to provide labour. The first actions in this order were to be in the south of the Lublin district in the area known as the

Zamość Lands. This area included Tomaszow Lubelski, just twenty miles from the town of Zamość.

This order was part of a much bigger plan; the complete germanisation of the whole Lublin district. The district was going to become the 'first resettlement area' of Generalplan Ost ('the General Plan for the East'). It was also intended to be the blueprint for the germanisation of all the occupied lands to the east of Germany, including Poland and the Russian territories as far as the Ural Mountains, which would then become the new border of the country.

The intention was that over time, Poland as a country would cease to exist. Hitler is quoted as saying in his 22 August 1939 speech to his Generals 'Poland will be depopulated and then settled by Germans . . . who, after all, speaks today of the annihilation of the Armenians?'

SS General Odilo Globocnik was appointed to be responsible for organising this plan. It was under his orders that the SS, assisted by collaborator forces like the Ukrainian Insurgent Army (UPA) carried out their work; the expulsion of all the Polish peasant farmers from the Zamość and Tomaszow counties and the collection of these people for forced labour in Berlin—an action that was to last from November 1942 to August 1943.

Homes and farms would be surrounded and without warning, occupants would be given five minutes to leave, many only had time to take bundles of blankets, clothes and some food. Meals were left half eaten as they were forced out. Hundreds escaped to the forests, but the Germans still managed to round up thousands and clear most of the farms and villages throughout the region.

The plan was that the whole region would then be colonised by SS men and their families and sixty thousand ethnic German families who would take advantage of the fertile black soil in the area.

In many cases, the farmers were rounded up, taken into the forests and shot. The UPA in particular responded to any Poles they encountered with extreme violence, carrying out numerous massacres. Over ten thousand Polish peasant farmers and villagers were murdered in the Zamość Lands clearances.

Joseph Poprzecznys' book 'Odilo Globocnik: Hitler's man in the East' makes reference to the clearances of the peasant farmers in the Tomaszow Lubelski area starting in December 1942 and carrying through to the summer and confirms the details I knew from my father that it was probably during these actions in 1943 that my father was taken from his family and his family uprooted and separated.

Those rounded up for forced labour at this time were taken to Zamość for processing. In 1939, Zamość had been a small town of about twenty eight thousand people, including twelve thousand Jews. After occupying the town, the Germans evicted the Jews from their homes and placed them in a ghetto. The town became a major hub of German activity.

The Jews were forced to provide labour to build an airfield and military barracks close to the town as well as two Russian prisoner of war camps. By November 1942, they had also built two transit camps in preparation to hold the captured peasants farmers as they were being processed.

When the construction work had been completed, the Germans liquidated the ghetto sending the Jews to Belzec. In one incident over five hundred men, women and children were shot dead in the streets as they were herded together in preparation for the journey.

The Germans created an extermination centre in the Zamość Rotunda, an old military arsenal south of the city and murdered over eight thousand people there, including many of the displaced peasant farmers and groups of Russian prisoners of war. In one incident a witness recalled thirty nine boy scouts and a group of boys wearing school uniform being shot as they sang the Polish national anthem.

Right: Polish Peasant farmers being rounded up in the Zamość region, Dec 1942.   *Left: Zamość Rotunda, site of eight thousand executions.*
(Photo sources 38 and 39)

As the first of the peasant farmers arrived at the Zamość transit camps, they were subject to a racial selection process. This would decide what was going to happen to them. This was the process that my father would have had to go through. The selection was intended to separate them into four categories.

Category one included anyone they considered to be ethnic German, this category included the descendants of German immigrants. Captives in this group were selected to be registered in the 'Deutsche Volkliste' (German People's List).

There were four groups in this category, groups one and two related to those who were actively or passively German in their way of life, groups three and four related to those with German blood who had become either passively or actively Polish and who depending on their responses might be able to be re-germanised.

Groups one and two were automatically placed on the Volkliste, group three resettled to German areas to be germanised and group four, if they did not respond favourably to the interrogations, sent to concentration camps.

An example of this process was recorded in the Nuremberg Military Tribunals in 1947; Maria Lambucki from Tomaszow Lubelski who despite being of German blood was completely Polish in her outlook, she was listed to be sent to a concentration camp, her children taken from her, separated and then sent to Germany. She decided to sign the Volkliste and agreed to be germanised.

About four thousand peasant farmers processed in Zamość came into this category. Many of those who had been placed on the Volkliste would be conscripted into the fighting units of the German Army. These selections were also carried out throughout Poland and thousands of people on the `Volkliste` who considered themselves to be Polish were forced to fight against their country, the alternative was for them or their families to be sent to concentration camps.

Category two included anyone who displayed `Nordic Germanic` racial features, such as blond hair and blue eyes. This was considered to be an indication of them being a member of the superior `Aryan Race

Anyone in this category was considered suitable to be germanised, particularly the children. If older they would be interrogated to determine if they could be re-educated. Thirty thousand Polish children between the ages of two and fourteen were kidnapped for this purpose in the clearances.

A brass band was set up in the transit camp where they were to be separated from their parents with the music intended to silence out the cries and screams of the children and their mothers.

Over four thousand of these children were considered suitable to be germanised. They were separated from their families, subjected to more racial tests and then sent to Berlin where they were either given to German families or placed in boarding schools to be raised as Germans. Only eight hundred returned to their families after the war.

The fate of most of the other children has never been fully discovered. Many were sent to the concentration camp / death camp at Majdanek on the outskirts of Lublin. Several hundred others were sent to Auschwitz where records show they were killed by a phenol injection to the heart as soon as they arrived. Witnesses report the children crying for their mothers as they are placed on a stool to be killed in turn. Some of the remainder were brought up by Polish families but nearly all survivors lost contact with their birth families.

Category three included the one my father would have found himself in, those who had been captured aged between fourteen and sixty and who were fit enough to work. This was the largest category with over fifty thousand captives. They would be held for two to six weeks in freezing barracks, surrounded by barbed wire with only the bare floor to sleep on before they were transported the nine hundred miles to Berlin and forced labour.

Category four was for those aged under four or over sixty plus the disabled or sick; those selected in this category were transferred to Zwierzyniec another transit camp just outside of Zamość where some were sent to be resettled in Warsaw, but most were sent to die at Auschwitz or Majdanek.

The lack of medicine and food combined with their ages ensured they were more susceptible to disease and malnutrition. The number of captives dying in this camp was high. One witness recalled seeing between fifteen and thirty dead children and infants being removed every day.

Over seventy thousand Poles including my father were processed through these transit camps between November 1942 and the end of 1943.

As the round ups continued, hundreds of farming families escaped to the forests and joined up with the partisans already hiding there. With these increased numbers, the Resistance soon became strong enough to engage the Germans on more equal terms, something that was impossible before the clearances started.

Resistance numbers were also boosted from February to August 1943 by the tens of thousands fleeing the Ukrainian UPA's ethnic cleansing of the Galicia and Wolyn (Volhynia) provinces to the south-east of the Zamość Lands. These provinces were part of pre-war Poland but were now part of Ukraine in the area Russia had annexed in 1939. Thousands of Polish peasant farmers and villagers still lived there.

The Ukrainian UPA often with German support would move from village to village, round up everyone, men, women, children and kill them. Over fifty thousand ethnic Poles were murdered in these actions in a few months. Extreme levels of violence were used, village priests were crucified, farmers beheaded, throats cut, pregnant women raped and bayoneted along with their children.

My thoughts returned to a childhood memory when I recalled a school friends' Polish father telling us how he saw SS soldiers throwing babies in the air and then catching them on their bayonets as they cleansed the village where he lived.

The Resistance were now fighting three enemies; the German Army, the ethnic German settlers and the Ukrainian Police and Paramilitary forces.

The two main Resistance groups at this time were the Bataliony Chlopskie (Bch or Peasant Battalions) created by the Agrarian Polish People's party in 1940 and the Armia Krajowa (AK or Home Army) which had been formed in 1942 from the surviving remnants of the pre-war Polish Army. These groups were originally created to provide self-defense, sabotage enemy plans and to prepare for a future national uprising but now started to engage the enemy forces in offensive actions.

From early 1943 through to 1944, the Home Army engaged the UPA in an attempt to protect ethnic Poles from the slaughter as the Galicia and Wolyn conflict spread over the border into the south Lublin counties of Zamość and Tomaszow Lubelski. The UPA believed these areas should also be part of an independent Ukraine.

The UPA were armed, trained and supported by the SS which ensured an effective fighting unit. I recalled my fathers' comments relating to his fear and dislike of the Russians / Ukrainians and could understand now why he felt what he did!

The UPA were a nationalist force, who by collaborating with the Germans and then ethnically cleansing the land they considered to be Ukrainian and by assisting the SS in the Zamość clearances, believed they would speed up the process of declaring an independent Ukraine after the war.

Despite the Resistance, the Germans had still been successful in rounding up over fifty thousand Poles in these actions and sending them back to Berlin. Many of those taken from this area were young peasant farm boys, just sixteen or seventeen years old who, like my father, had never been away from home before. The deportations continued throughout most of 1943.

The plan to germanise the area was also still going to plan and by the summer of 1943 the Germans had expelled most of the Poles. One hundred and seventy villages had been completely cleared and the first group of eight thousand ethnic Germans settled in the houses and farms taken from the Poles.

As the Germans tried to colonise the area, the settlers became the target of the partisans and many were killed including a hundred and fifty settlers in one incident alone. Twelve thousand partisans were now based in the dense forests around Zamość and another two thousand in the forests outside of Tomaszow Lubelski.

The German army was also coming under increasing pressure as the intensity and number of attacks increased, trains were derailed, bridges and railway tracks blown up and German soldiers subject to a series of hit-and-run attacks and ambushes. The Germans reprisals in the area were brutal with many villages in the area destroyed and villagers executed.

By June 1943, the Resistance was proving so effective that the Germans decided to carry out a major anti partisan operation, the *Wehrwolf Action* to bring the area back under their control. Thirty thousand battle experienced SS troops were ordered into the area in an attempt to take control of the forests. They engaged the partisans in several battles with both sides suffering high losses but the Germans were never able to completely clear the forests.

Despite losing more than half their men, the partisans remained defiant and continued to harass the invading troops and attack any German settlers. This ensured that the Germans were never able to fully control the Zamość lands and that the plan to colonise the area failed. It also ensured that further large scale forced labour deportations from this area ceased by the end of 1943.

The defence of the Zamość Lands became one of the largest and most successful actions of the Resistance during the war and became known as the Zamość Uprising.

*By 1943 many Partisan groups based in forests were now fighting back throughout Poland.
Left: Jedrusie Partisans active around Krakow and in central Poland.
Right: Polish and Jewish Partisans, Yanov Forest, Lublin.
(Photo sources 40 and 41)*

My father was taken from his family sometime in the first six months of 1943. He was then either transported by lorry or marched in a group to Zamość to be processed. When he had been taken from his home, he managed to find some photographs of his mother and his family to bring with him.

At Zamość, he was placed in the category considered suitable for forced labour, before being transported by train to Berlin with thousands of others. The conditions on these trains were desperate; the captives had little space and were crammed into freezing cattle cars with no food or water. Some died on the journey.

All along this journey, the trains would pass burnt-out carriages and human bodies left lying by the tracks, all of which could be seen from the cars. One lasting memory my father once commented on was of the constant sound of planes overhead.

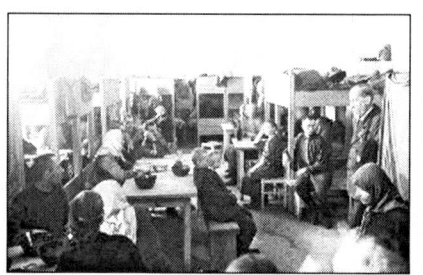

Crowded forced-labour barracks in Germany. Men, women and children were kept together. (Photo sources 42 and 43)

On arriving in Berlin, they disembarked the cattle cars into a transit camp where they were registered for work by German officials and then allocated a range of jobs. Many were assigned to the munitions and armaments factories, others were allocated to farms to ensure food supply needs could be met and still others were sent to jobs in the construction industry to build fortifications, repair bomb damage and rebuild roads.

The workers were forced to work seven days a week with minimal food rations usually based on bread and vegetable soup. Up to three thousand workers were held in barracks built close to the main factories in different cities to ensure a ready labour force.

By the middle of 1943, the German Army was beginning to suffer huge losses particularly on the Russian front. The Germans replaced many of these losses with those ethnic Germans registered on the Volkliste.

Many of these new conscripts were then sent to fight on the Russian Front, where life expectancy was very short. The Western and Italian Fronts were considered the easier option as they believed the fighting to be less brutal, many of these soldiers planned to surrender to the Allies at the first opportunity.

Surrendering to the Russians was not an option, as the Russians routinely executed prisoners. Desertion was a risk as any deserters would be shot if they were caught and the threat to send families to concentration camps if they deserted still existed.

By September 1943, the Allies had landed in Italy and were forcing their way up through the country. The Germans needed to maintain an effective supply line from Berlin to the Italian front line.

To organise this, the transport section of the German Army, the *Transportkorps Speer*, conscripted forced labourers to work as auxiliaries to drive supply trucks to the front line. The first task was to teach the young labourers how to drive, as few already knew how to do so.

This is what happened to my father, now aged just eighteen, he was taught how to drive and provided with a driving licence. He was then, along with twenty thousand mainly Polish and Russian prisoners forced to drive supply trucks from Berlin through the Alps and into northern Italy to the German forces facing the Allies. As the Allied advance intensified, this job became very dangerous, as air raids targeted the supply routes and these supply convoys.

General Anders and Scenes from the Battle of Monte Cassino—1944

Left: General Wladyslaw Anders. Middle: Polish Second Corps cap badge. Right: Polish War Memorial overlooking Monte Cassino. General Anders was buried at the Polish cemetery at Monte Cassino in 1970
(Photo sources 44, 45, 46)

Left and Right: Polish Troops fighting at Monte Cassino.
(Photo sources 47 and 48)

Left: Polish troops preparing to fire. Right: Polish tanks at Monte Cassino.
(Photo sources 49 and 50)

The Allied invasion of Italy, led by the US Fifth Army and British Eighth Army, was aided by the Polish Second Corps, consisting of seventy thousand men. This Army included the remnants of the Polish forces that had fought in the Battles at Tomaszow Lubelski in September 1939 and had managed to escape to Romania and thousands of the prisoners captured by the Russians from the occupied lands after the Russian invasion of Poland.

These prisoners had been released after British negotiations with the Russians succeeded in convincing them that the Allies needed more manpower to defeat the Germans after the German invasion of Russia in 1941. These survivors added to the Polish Army of the East, which had been fighting since the beginning of the war through Persia, Egypt and North Africa before they combined with other Polish regiments to form the Polish Second Corps in 1943.

This Army was now led by General Wladyslaw Anders, who had commanded a cavalry brigade during the Battle of Tomaszow before being wounded, captured and then tortured by the Russians. The Russians agreed to release him to take charge of this new regiment. This force became known as Anders' Army as a tribute to his leadership.

The Allied advance through Italy was difficult, as these forces faced elite and battle-hardened German troops who had organised strong defences at every stage including the impregnable old monastery at Monte Cassino.

The Germans had been able to hold the Allied advance through three battles at this location until May 1944. At that point, after fierce hand-to-hand fighting, the Polish troops fighting alongside the Allies were finally able to break through the German defences and raise the Polish flag over the abbey, an achievement now recognised as one of Poland's greatest military successes.

The defeat of the stronghold at Monte Cassino opened the road north to Rome. The Poles then took a leading part in battles for Ancona in July 1944 and Bologna in April 1945. These victories were crucial to the Allies' success in the war as these battles, along with the toppling of Mussolini and Fascist Italy in July 1943, allowed the Allies to concentrate all their manpower on Germany.

By early 1945, the Allies were aware of the Russian advances on the Eastern Front and the liberation of concentration camps in the German-occupied territories. This development was to become crucial as it was also a sign to any forced labourers and Poles conscripted into the German Army that the threat to family members back home of being sent to these camps no longer existed.

As the invasion continued north, the Allies encountered more and more Polish forced labourers and / or soldiers who had deserted the German Army. Many of them were found hiding in the countryside.

After processing the first few escapees, the Polish Second Corps command became aware that many thousands of the German auxiliary drivers in Italy were actually Polish nationals either forcibly conscripted into the *Transportkorps Speer*, or being used as forced labour. They also became aware that there were also a significant number of Poles forcibly conscripted into the fighting units of the German Army.

General Anders decided that this was a good opportunity to boost recruitment, particularly as the Russians were now refusing to allow further recruitment from within the areas of Poland they controlled. They feared a strong Polish Army would cause them problems in the future.

He wanted to make sure any Poles on the German side of the front line became aware that the Polish Army was on the other side and to encourage them to try and escape and join them in the fight against the Germans.

It was decided that the best way to do this was by dropping thousands of leaflets from the air on to the German side of the front line and by sending out continuous radio messages. These radio messages included up to date news of developments in the war including the liberation of the camps in eastern Poland.

These messages also made it clear that if any Poles conscripted into the German Army managed to get away and were still worried about consequences for their families back home then they would be allowed to sign up with the Polish Army using false names.

> **Adapted content of messages dropped behind German lines to Poles forcibly conscripted into the German Army and auxiliary forces.**
>
> *The Americans, British, Canadians and French fight with our Polish Armed Forces.*
> *At the first opportunity, go to the Allied Forces or hide to wait for their arrival.*
> *The Allied Forces have been reliably informed about your situation.*
> *When you come into contact with them tell them you are Polish.*
> *If held with German prisoners ask to be separated.*
> *Ask to be put in contact with the Polish military authorities.*
> *Waiting for you are your brothers who are fighting alongside our Allies to liberate you.*
> *Long live Poland!*
>
> **(Photo Source 51)**

The next chapter in my father's life begins sometime during late 1944 or early 1945, as my mother told me. My father and another Polish driver were transporting supplies through Northern Italy when they encountered bomb-damaged roads which prevented them continuing their journey.

My father had seen two bicycles leaning against a wall in a village that they had just driven through. They had seen the leaflets dropped by the Polish Second Corps and decided that this was a good chance to get away, so they left the lorry, went back to the village, took the bicycles and then continued south with the intention of joining up with the Polish Army.

An Italian family hid them for a while, letting them sleep in a barn and feeding them in return for work on their farm until an opportunity came to cross over to the Allied side. My father said that the Italian family was very kind and had an attractive daughter, whom he liked.

He really appreciated what the family did, as it would have been dangerous for them to hide him and his companion as the Germans still controlled the area and would execute whole families of anyone helping escaped workers or deserters.

As the Allied advance continued, my father and his companion continued south, travelling mostly by night until they were picked up by American soldiers. As Poles, they were taken to Taranto to be processed where they were subject to an interrogation to determine that they were actually Polish and what their role was while under German control. This process was to determine whether they had any military training and what skills they might be able offer.

They were also keen to identify anyone who had served in the SS, they would be held separately and prevented from joining up. Those who passed through the processing were then taken to the Polish Second Corps base in San Basilio, where they were given uniforms. After signing an oath, they were conscripted into the Polish Army. This process lasted a few days before the new conscripts were sent to the front line.

My father had now joined the remnants of the same army he had seen defeated five years earlier as a fourteen-year-old boy nearly fifteen hundred miles away back home in Tomaszow.

The Polish Second Corps had been in some of the fiercest fighting of the campaign and, by the autumn of 1944, had become desperately short of manpower. The plan to enlist escaped Polish forced labourers proved successful, and eleven thousand conscripts including my father joined up in the early months of 1945.

This recruitment drive was so successful that it was expanded to the Western Front, where another fifty-four thousand Poles who had also been held by the Germans managed to cross over to join other Polish armies by early 1945.

My father must have obtained a camera around this time as in the suitcase I found in the attic were numerous photographs of him at Monte Cassino, Taranto and other locations in Italy as well with Polish Army colleagues.

Left: Monte Cassino after the battle. Right: A tank from the battle. My fathers' photographs.

Documents and my father's photographs show that he was now a private in the Polish Second Corps. I am unsure of what he experienced in the army, as he never spoke about what happened except to say that he drove a tank. His paperwork also indicates that he was in the armoured division.

The American and Allied forces continued their march towards Berlin from the west and with the Russians successfully advancing from the east ensured the final collapse of Germany and its surrender on 7 May 1945. My father was still only nineteen years old.

My fathers' photographs of Polish Army in Italy after the end of the war.

As the war ended the men of the Polish Second Corps were instructed to stay in Italy and carry out general occupational duties which included helping the local police in law enforcement and guarding German prisoners of war. This lasted for over a year.

The soldiers in the Corps now numbered over a hundred thousand and many of the young soldiers like my father finally had the chance to relax and enjoy the Italian sun and meet local girls now that the war was over.

My father (on left) in Italy after the end of the war.

The Poles had developed a good reputation as a powerful fighting unit and were well thought of by the British, American and Commonwealth troops they had fought with, but by 1946 they were now facing a situation they could not win; the impact of all the political changes that had been made in Eastern Europe.

In the background, major decisions were being considered about what was going to happen to them and to the future of Poland as a country. With the war now over, the thousands of soldiers in the Polish Second Corps had been looking forward to returning to their free homeland and being reunited with their families or what was left of them.

However, hopes of returning home to Poland were not to be!

What happened in Tomaszow was the same as what happened to thousands of other Polish cities, towns and villages. Tens of thousands of Poles shared similar stories to my father. Poland suffered a higher percentage of casualties during World War II than any other country in Europe, with nearly 22 per cent of the population, nearly six million people being killed.

Hitler made his intentions for the Polish people very clear in a speech given on 22 August 1939 in which he ordered his forces 'to kill without pity or mercy all men, women and children of the Polish race or language. Only in such a way will we win the vital living space that we need.'

His intention was to reduce Poland to a country fit only to provide manual labour for their German masters. To do this, he attempted to destroy anything to do with Polish history and culture. He targeted the Polish educated class or *Intelligentsia,* believing that by destroying it, the country would be easier to control with no leaders.

Tens of thousands of priests, professors, teachers, doctors, lawyers, journalists and educated people were executed or sent to concentration camps, where many later died. To prevent the rise of educated Poles in the future, he banned the use of the Polish language, he closed schools and universities and decreed that Polish children would receive only the most basic education, teaching them only simple mathematics and to write their names. Reading was not considered necessary.

The enormity and magnitude of what happened to the Jews during the war has made it possible to almost overlook the fact that in addition to murdering three million Polish Jews, the Germans also murdered nearly three million Polish Christians in what has became known as 'the forgotten Holocaust'.

Although Hitler had planned the systematic extermination of the whole Jewish race, his plan relating to the 'Slav and Polish problem' was to be more long term; through mass executions and mass deportations of the Polish people, he hoped to first remove any Polish culture from the country and then completely germanise it by resettling it with ethnic Germans.

The plan was that over time the Polish race would eventually cease to exist. He planned to deport up to 20 million Poles to slave labour camps in Western Siberia where most would be expected to die. The Germans believed that because the Poles were such a patriotic and proud people that they could not easily be integrated into this new Germany and this was the only solution.

The failure to successfully settle ethnic Germans in the Lublin, Zamość and Tomaszow regions, in part due to the 'Zamość Uprising' ensured that the Germans were never able to achieve the first stage of this plan.

Apart from an occasional one-line comment, my father would never speak about what happened during the war and would only say how lucky he was to still be alive when so many others had died. His home town of Tomaszow had been almost totally destroyed. Only about four thousand of the town's original twelve thousand inhabitants had survived the war.

Back in Tomaszow, the Russians, allies of the West since 1941, had liberated the town in July 1944. The following year, the Russian NKVD and the UB (Polish secret police) established a prison there to house and execute soldiers of the Polish Home Army and Peasants' Battalions, believing them to be loyal to the Polish government in exile. This prison, also known as the Dragon's Den, continued its operations, imprisoning or executing anyone who opposed the new Communist government until 1956.

In one of the most ignoble acts of the war, the British and American leaders, tired of six years of war, signed the Yalta Treaty on 11 February 1945, to appease the Russians. Under this treaty, the Russians were allowed to annex the Polish land that they had already taken in 1939.

The effect of this would determine what was going to happen to all the Polish forces in Europe. The Poles soon realised that they would not be able to return to the free Poland they had been fighting for. Most members of the Polish armed forces considered this a complete betrayal of their country, despite this they continued to be an effective and committed fighting force throughout the Italian campaign and on the Western Front.

The Polish government in exile based in London, had wanted to maintain its army in Britain as an active fighting unit so it could return home to fight for a free Poland, but without the support of the west, this could not happen.

General Anders was deprived of his Polish citizenship and military rank in 1946 by the interim Communist government and was exiled to London, where he remained active in the affairs of the government in exile and as the Inspector General of the Polish Second Corps in the resettlement programme. His Polish citizenship and military rank were eventually re-instated in 1989 after the collapse of Communism, nineteen years after his death.

A new Communist government was set up in Poland under Russian control in January 1947. When Britain decided to recognise this new government at the expense of the Polish government in exile, many Poles, including my father felt devastated at what the consequences of this decision would be.

Russia then insisted that all its nationals including anyone from the newly annexed territories had to be sent back to Russia. They also stated that anyone born within its territories, including the new lands was by definition a Russian citizen. This now included thirty thousand soldiers in the Polish Second Corps who now found that their pre-war homes were now in Russia and not Poland.

The new Polish Communist government also insisted that all the Polish forces abroad should be placed under the command of the country's new government and that they should be immediately returned to Poland in their divisions.

The British authorities originally were keen for the Poles to be returned home, however there was a high level of Polish Army opposition to this plan. It soon became clear that any soldiers who had fought for their country or who were loyal to the old government in exile were at risk of death or imprisonment if they were returned home. The level of opposition ensured that the British Government would re-evaluate its plans for the repatriation of Poles.

There were some forced repatriations and a number of Poles and East Europeans were sent back to their home countries where they were persecuted by the ruling Communist regimes. In some cases, particularly those involving the Cossacks and Ukrainians, repatriation ended up with hundreds being executed for treason with many more being sent to gulags and labour camps in Siberia. As the repatriations continued there were many cases of suicide, including thirty officers of the Polish Second Corps, who killed themselves rather than return home.

In the end the British government decided they would not enforce the repatriation of the Second Corps, a deciding factor in this decision was the strong bond of mutual trust that had developed between the men of the British Eighth Army and the Second Corps. The government called this a moral decision.

My father told me they were then given a choice of whether they wanted to settle in Britain, any of the Commonwealth countries or the United States. They were also given the option of returning to Poland or Russia.

The number who did not want to return to Poland and who wanted to come to Britain was so high that the British government set up a separate organisation to help them settle in this country; the Polish Resettlement Corps which was created in 1946 to help them learn about Britain and to integrate them into the British way of life.

By not standing up to the Russians at Yalta, the Western Allies enabled Russia to set up a series of Communist regimes in most of Eastern Europe. These countries provided a buffer zone between Russia and the West and ensured years of military and nuclear tension between the two ideologies.

After failing to support Poland at the beginning of the war, my father and most of his army colleagues now saw this as the second time that Poland had been betrayed by the West. He also believed that most of the men in the Second Corps would have preferred to return home to Poland and would have done so had the circumstances been different.

From my fathers' point of view, he had said that he had always intended to return to his family in Tomaszow; however he was not sure if he had any family left or even a home to return to. After he had been deported to Germany, It seemed likely that his family would have been separated and uprooted during the ethnic cleansing of the Zamość Lands in 1943. At the time there did not seem to be anyway to find out what had actually happened.

He had also been told it would be dangerous to return because the new Communist government were imprisoning or executing anyone who had been in the Polish forces or who had expressed loyalty to the Polish government in exile. My father recalled his fear of the Russians and what they were capable of and when he was told that the Russian secret police, the NKVD were active in the Tomaszow area, he became very wary about returning home.

Left: My father on the right in Italy.   Right: My father leaving Italy for England, February 1947.

Taking all these factors into consideration and combined with his memories of how difficult life had been in a poverty stricken pre-war

Tomaszow, let alone what the struggle would be in a war-ravaged Poland, he made his choice and decided to come to England to start a new life. My father was then shipped off to England at the beginning of 1947 with thousands of other displaced people and refugees.

They disembarked onto English soil with just the clothes they stood up in and a few belongings. In my father's case, this included the small suitcase I found in the attic. No one knew where their lives would end up or whether they would ever see their families or homes again.

My father never saw his family again!

After arriving in England, my father and other Polish Second Corps soldiers were conscripted into the newly established Polish Resettlement Corps. Former army and air force camps were used for accommodation. By the end of 1947, one hundred and fourteen thousand Polish soldiers were living in two hundred and sixty five camps throughout the country, mostly in rural areas. These numbers increased as family members also arrived.

The government also passed the 'Polish Resettlement Act' in 1947 which became the first ever mass immigration legislation in Britain. The act was passed on the basis that the Poles were a special case due to the respect held for its soldiers by the British command and was not available to other nationalities or groups of refugees.

The act gave the Poles the right to work as well as unemployment assistance if needed and ensured they could access all aspects of British life including health care and education.

The Resettlement Corps was designed to keep the conscripts under military control until they adjusted to civilian life; they were expected to sign up for two years. The refugees were spread all around the country with the intention of integrating them into local communities. Members of the Corps were still subject to British military discipline and law.

My father and the other members of the Corps were given National Identity Registration cards, National Insurance numbers and Food Ration books. They had to keep these papers on their person at all times, along with their stamped Alien Registration certificate which provided evidence of their right to be in England.

My father at the resettlement camp in England, about 1948.

They were then allocated beds in the Nissen huts which were to become their homes for the foreseeable future. Families were provided with curtained-off areas in these huts, while single men were provided only with beds organised in a dormitory style with little or no privacy. These displaced-persons camps were very basic, with limited heating and poor cooking facilities. My father did recall how good it felt to be safe and how grateful he was that he had been provided with a starting point for the next stage of his life.

Although the Polish Resettlement Corps officially disbanded in 1949, three displaced-persons camps remained until the early 1960s. Some Poles spent more than fifteen years in these camps, some older men particularly found it difficult to integrate and learn new skills, but most left as soon as they could find work.

My father was provided with accommodation in a camp at Oulton Park in Cheshire, before moving to the Lichfield area in the Midlands. The soldiers were given daily lessons in English as well as basic training in a range of jobs to make them employable.

AN ORDINARY POLISH BOY

The members of the Resettlement Corps could only leave the camps if they could get work. The Corp helped organise job interviews and once they had managed to get work, they were allowed to leave the army and start new lives as civilians. They were however, still part of the Corps Reserve until they had completed their two years of service. To ensure a smooth transition into British life, they would be recalled to the Corps and the camp if they lost their jobs for any reason.

Left: Nissen hut living quarters.

Right: Polish soldiers at Oulton Park Resettlement Camp, 1948.

When they became civilians, they were still subject to lots of conditions. Travel to other towns was forbidden without special permission, and they had to notify the police of any changes of address. They also had to report to the local police station on a regular basis to get their Alien Registration certificates stamped.

It wasn't until 1960, after nearly thirteen years of living in England that that my father finally had his Registration certificate stamped to indicate he was now allowed to move freely within the country and that he was no longer required to register regularly with the police.

My father used to comment on there being lots of prejudice from local people about foreigners taking work from them. Although people still had sympathy for what had happened to Poland and its people, times were hard and jobs were not easy to get with thousands of returning soldiers also looking for work.

There was even an anti-Polish campaign by the Trades Unions which turned public opinion against the Poles. However, most of the hostility subsided after negotiations between the unions and the government succeeded.

The British authorities were keen for the soldiers to lose their 'foreignness' and embrace British customs. One example of this was they forbid the flying of Polish flags in the camps believing that it was counter-productive to them being absorbed into British civilian life.

My father had been conscripted into the Resettlement Corps from February 1947 and after completed a basic mechanics course with the Corps succeeded in finding work as a mechanic's assistant with 'Hollinshead and Sons' garage on Beacon Street in Lichfield on 16 July 1948.

He was then able to leave the Polish Army and start a new life as a civilian in his new country. He did however remain in the Corps Reserve as he was required to do until February 1949, when he was finally demobbed.

Within eighteen months of enlisting in the Corps over three quarters of the men had managed to find employment. On the whole, most Poles integrated well into English society and gained a reputation as good workers, particularly in the construction, farming and the manual-labour jobs needed to rebuild the country. Most of them built successful and constructive lives in their new country.

My father continued to work at the garage until October 1953, when he got permission to move to take up a welding job in Wolverhampton, where he met my mother at a local dance.

My mother, Wendy Meates, was English from the seaside town of Swanage in Dorset. She had been evacuated to the Midlands for a time during the war after her fourteen-year-old brother had been injured by shrapnel while doing a paper round in a south coast bombing raid in 1942. She returned to the area after the war to work and ended up meeting my father.

My mother and father in 1956 . . .

After a short courtship, my parents married in 1954, and I was born in Wolverhampton in June 1955, and my sister, Tina, was born in August 1956. Home was a one-room attic at the top of forty stairs with a shared bathroom and fruit boxes covered with linen for furniture.

The post-war world was so different from the world of today. The struggle to survive that many people faced seems impossible for young people now to fully appreciate. I can still remember the ice that built up on the inside of the windows at home and the house always being freezing cold in winter. Few people in those days could afford proper heating. Most of our clothing was second-hand or repaired, and the garden was always full of junk as nothing would ever be thrown out in case it would be useful one day.

This was how my father's life started in England.

Afterword

My family moved to Bristol in 1958, and my father worked as a welder there until he retired in 1990. He always enjoyed bonfire night. I still don't believe it was a Polish custom that you had to hold the fireworks, which he did as he let them off, and I don't know how we managed to survive having twenty lit candles on the Christmas tree every year, another Polish custom, I was told.

He was always proud of being Polish and always liked to wear his army beret with the Polish Second Corps badge whenever he was working. He decided it was important for him to retain his Polish nationality and refused the opportunity to become naturalised as a British citizen when the suggestion came up, even after nearly fifty years in the country.

My father was never able to fully retire from work, and he continued to work every day in his garage repairing cars until he died in 1996 at age seventy-one. Although I never really got to know anything about what he really thought, the legacy he leaves me is his incredible work ethic: he was never out of work, never went on holiday and never had a day off. He always continued the job until it was finished, however long it took, there was, however, only one way to do any job, his way, which did make for some very interesting mechanical and electrical repairs in our family home.

He never did see his family again, although he did manage to make contact with one brother, Tomasz, in the early 1950s. Tomasz was still living in the Tomaszow area and was struggling to make a living as a farmer. He and my father lost contact with each other again soon after. My father also discovered that his sister and mother were also alive at the time and living somewhere in Russia, but he was not able to trace them.

The political situation between Russia and the West ensured that he never had the opportunity to meet his family again, and his mother died never again seeing the young boy who had been taken from her so many years previously. He was never able to find out what had happened to his other brother or his father.

My mother retired back to Swanage in 1997 and continues to live there. Both my sister and I and our families still enjoy regular trips to the seaside to see her and enjoy the charms of this beautiful town.

FOOTNOTE

I knew Germany had invaded Poland on 1 September 1939, and as a child growing up, I also knew that Britain and France had declared war on Germany on the 3 September in response to the invasion, but I was unaware that despite declaring war, Britain and France actually did nothing to support or help Poland in its hour of need. The Polish Army had retreated and regrouped near Tomaszow to wait for the Western support that had been promised, and the Russian Army held back, unsure of Western commitment.

No one at the time expected this to develop into a major war

By 17 September, nearly three weeks after Germany had invaded, with no action or support from France or Britain (as stipulated by their treaty), Russia believed the West's commitment was weak and gained the confidence to attack the Poles from the east and support the Germans.

This ensured the Polish defeat at the Battle of Tomaszow Lubelski, which lasted from 17 to 26 September, and the collapse of Poland. The rest is history. I knew my father felt betrayed by Britain's and France's lack of action, but I could not, as a child, understand why.

Unlike most other European countries, Poland never surrendered. Its armies, with more than two hundred fifty thousand troops, was the fourth largest army in Europe throughout the conflict, and they fought in every theatre of war, gaining a reputation as a formidable fighting force with successes through Persia, Egypt, North Africa, Italy, Germany and Scandinavia. The bravery of Polish pilots ensured Britain won the Battle of Britain.

> **What would have happened if Britain and France had mobilised earlier as they were committed to do within the terms of the British-Polish Common Defence Pact signed in August 1939?**
>
> Some military historians have concluded that an immediate, forceful military response from Britain and France could probably have prevented the whole world war, as Russia would not have attacked the Polish Army and enabled the Germans to defeat Poland, and Germany's western borders, with no defences (as its armies were committed in Poland), would have crumbled easily if attacked. The lack of support for Poland enabled the situation to escalate as it did and provided conditions for Russian dominance in Eastern Europe and the Cold War.

Sources of Information

My story is based on following a timeline of what happened in the locations my father found himself in on his journey to England. I have listed the sources of information in a sequential order of this journey.

All numbers and statistics have been sourced from many of the sites listed. In recent years, the Polish Institute of National Remembrance has been re-evaluating many of these figures and is in the process of collating evidence to determine exactly what happened in the war years and how many people were killed or taken into exile as figures can vary depending on the source.

Invasion of Poland:

- Invasion of Poland', Wikipedia, http://en.wikipedia.org/wiki/Invasion_of_Poland, accessed Dec. 2010.

- 'The September Campaign', Polish Greatness [blog], http://www.polishgreatness.com/septembercampaign.html, accessed Dec. 2010.

- `The Polish September Campaign 1939` Poland in Exile http://www.polandinexile.com/army1.htm

- Karski Jan, Story of a Secret State: My Report to the World Publisher: (Penguin—5 May 2011)

History of Tomaszow Lubelski:

- 'History of Tomaszow Lubelski', http://tomaszow.info/, accessed Dec. 2010.

- 'History of Tomaszow Lubelski', http://www.tomaszow-lubelski.pl/.

- Morris Gradel, 'Tomaszow Lubelski', *Encyclopaedia of Jewish Communities in Poland*, http://www.jewishgen.org/yizkor/pinkas_poland/pol7_00237b.html.

- 'Tomaszow Lubelski', http://www.jewishvirtuallibrary.org/jsource/judaica/ejud_0002_0020_0_19937.html

- 'Tomaszow Lubelski', Wikipedia, http://en.wikipedia.org/wiki/Tomasz%C3%B3w_Lubelski, accessed 27 Dec. 2010.

- 'Tomaszow Lubelski', http://www.sztetl.org.pl/en/city/tomaszow-lubelski/

- `The Tomaszow Lubelski Community`, http://tomashov.org.il/english/community

- 'Testimony of Wajsleder Chana-Szpizajren', http://tomashov.org.il/testimonies/5786.

Battle of Tomaszow Lubelski:

- 'Battle of Tomaszow Lubelski', Wikipedia, http://en.wikipedia.org/wiki/Battle_of_Tomasz%C3%B3w_Lubelski, accessed Dec. 2010.

- 'Battle of Tomaszow Lubelski', *Total War Center* [discussion forum], http://www.twcenter.net/forums/showthread.php?t=197146. accessed Dec. 2010.

- 'Battle of Tomaszow Lubelski', *Polish Greatness* [blog], accessed Dec. 2010.http://www.polishgreatness.com/battlesofworldwartwo.html.

- 'Sept. 17, 1939: Battle of Tomaszow Lubelski', *1939* [blog], http://war1939.blogspot.co.uk/2009/06/sept-17-1939-battle-of-tomaszow.html. accessed Jan. 2011

Katyn Massacre:

- 'Katyn massacre', Wikipedia, http://en.wikipedia.org/wiki/Katyn_massacre, accessed Jan. 2011.

- 'Katyn Forest Massacre', http://www.katyn.org.au/, accessed Jan. 2011.

- 'Soviet repressions of Polish citizens', Wikipedia, http://en.wikipedia.org/wiki/Soviet_repressions_of_Polish_citizens, accessed Oct. 2012.

- 'The Katyn Wood Massacre', *History Learning Site*, http://www.historylearningsite.co.uk/katyn_wood_massacre.htm.

- 'Polska 1939-1945: Straty Osobowe I Ofiary Represji Pod Dwiema Okupaciami', http://niniwa2.cba.pl/polska_1939_1945.htm.

Belzec Labour and Death Camps:

- 'Labour Camps—Belzec, Sobibor and Treblinka ', Holocaust Research http://www.holocaustresearchproject.org/ar/labour20camps/arclabourcamps.html

- 'Belzec Death Camp', http://www.holocaustresearchproject.org/ar/belzec.html

- 'Belzec Overview', Aktion Reinhard Camps, www.deathcamps.org/belzec/.

- 'Belzec Labour camps', Aktion Reinhard Camps, www.deathcamps.org/belzec/labourcamps.html.

- 'Belzec', Jewish Virtual Library, www.jewishvirtuallibrary.org/jsource/Holocaust/Belzec.

- 'Belzec extermination camp', Wikipedia, http://en.wikipedia.org/wiki/Belzec_extermination_camp, accessed Feb. 2011.

- 'Belzec (Poland)', *Jewish Gen*, http://www.jewishgen.org/forgottenCamps/Camps/BelzecEng.html.

- 'Extermination camps', Wikipedia, http://en.wikipedia.org/wiki/Extermination_camp, accessed June 2011

- 'Hell of Belzec Death Camp', http://auschwitz.dk/belzec.htm.

- 'Holocaust', 'Belzec', History Learning Site, accessed Feb 2011 http://www.historylearningsite.co.uk/belzec.htm

- 'The Holocaust', Wikipedia, http://en.wikipedia.org/wiki/The_Holocaust, accessed June 2011.

- Yitzhak Arad, Belzec, Sobibor,Treblinka: The Operation Reinhard Death Camps. (Indiana University Press; New edition—1 Jun 1999)

- `Belzec` A film by Guillaume Moscovitz produced by Menemsha Films 2005

The 'Einsatzgruppen':

- 'Babi Yar', *The Berdichev Revival*, http://www.berdichev.org/babi_yar.htm.

- 'Babi Yar', Wikipedia, http://en.wikipedia.org/wiki/Babi_Yar, accessed June 2011.

- `Einsatzgruppen', Wikipedia, http://en.wikipedia.org/wiki/Einsatzgruppen, accessed June 2011.

- 'Einsatzgruppen', *USHMM*, http://www.ushmm.org/wlc/en/article.php?ModuleId.

- 'Einsatzgruppen', *ARC*, http://www.deathcamps.org/occupation/einsatzgruppen.html.

- 'Einsatzgruppen', *Jewish Virtual Library*, http://www.jewishvirtuallibrary.org/jsource/Holocaust/einsatztoc.html.

- 'Testimony of Rivka Yosilevska' `Genocide', *World at War*, Episode 20, Thames TV, 3 March 1974.

- Rudolf Schlossberg ` The Einsatzgruppen` B005KO6EDI Amazon Media EU S.à r.l. (1 Sep 2011)

Zamosc:

- `Massacres of Poles in Volhynia and Eastern Galicia`, Wikipedia, http://en.wikipedia.org/wiki/Massacres_of_Poles_in_Volhynia accessed Dec. 2012

- `Opening Statement of the Prosecution, Nuremburg` (Case 8: 'RuSHA Case'), Axis History Forum, http://forum.axishistory.com/viewtopic.php?t=56404

- 'Zamosc Ghetto', *Holocaust Research Project*, http://www.holocaustresearchproject.org/ghettos/zamosc.html.

- 'Zamosc Uprising', *International Research Centre*, http://www.internationalresearchcenter.org/en/euhttp://culture.polishsite.us/articles/art4.

- 'Zamosc During the World War II & Roztocze National Park', *Polish Culture Site*, http://culture.polishsite.us/articles/art403.html. accessed Dec. 2012

- 'Zamosc Uprising', Wikipedia, http://en.wikipedia.org/wiki/Zamo%C5%9B%C4%87_Uprising. accessed Dec. 2012.

- `Zamosc`, http://www.jewishvirtuallibrary.org/jsource/judaica/ejud_0002_0021_0_21390.html

- "Zamosc"—Encyclopedia of Jewish Communities in Poland, Volume VII http://www.jewishgen.org/Yizkor/pinkas_poland/pol7_00203.html

- Joseph Poprzeczny, `Odilo Globocnik: Hitler's Man in the East` (Jefferson, N Carolina and London. McFarland & Company Inc. 2004)

- Richard C. Lukas `Did the Children Cry? Hitler's War against Jewish and Polish Children, 1939-1945`. (Hippocrene Books, New York, 2001.) http://www.projectinposterum.org/docs/lucas2.htm

The Forced Labour Programme:

- 'Albert Speer', Wikipedia, http://en.wikipedia.org/wiki/Albert_Speer, accessed Oct. 2012.

- 'Albert Speer', *GlobalSecuirty.org*, http://www.globalsecurity.org/military/world/europe/de-speer.htm, accessed Oct. 2012.

- 'Forced Labour under German Rule during World War II', Wikipedia, http://en.wikipedia.org/wiki/Forced_labour_under_German_rule_during_World_War_II, accessed Sept. 2012.

- Jeanne Dingell, 'Polish Forced Laborers', 1998, http://www.thornb2b.co.uk/P/P_docs/dingell.pdf, accessed Sept. 2012.

- 'The Fate of Poles Forcibly Conscripted into German Army', http://www.wehrmacht-polacy.pl/, accessed Oct. 2012.

- 'Poles in the Wehrmacht', Wikipedia, http://en.wikipedia.org/wiki/Poles_in_the_Wehrmacht, accessed Sept. 2012

- 'Poles in the German Army', http://brozbar.cieplowizja.pl/mapy/brozbar24/przymusowi/ index.html&usg=ALkJrhh9QmoiNs1El29lWldvoXycYB-A_Q.

- 'The Slave Labor Program', Yale Law School Lillian Goldman Law Library, http://avalon.law.yale.edu/imt/chap10.asp

- 'Transportkorps Speer', Wikipedia, http://de.wikipedia.org/wiki/Transportkorps_Speer, accessed Oct. 2012.

Italy:

- 'Contribution of the Poles in the Italian Campaign', *Monte Cassino Battlefield Tour*, http://nuke.montecassinotour.com/

- 'Spring Offensive', Wikipedia, http://en.wikipedia.org/wiki/Spring_1945_offensive_in_Italy, accessed Oct. 2012.

- The contribution of Anders army at Monte Cassino/tabid/79/Default.aspx.

- 'Italian Campaign', Wikipedia, http://en.wikipedia.org/wiki/Italian_Campaign_ (World_War_II), accessed Oct. 2012.

- 'II Corps (Poland)', http://en.wikipedia.org/wiki/II_Corps_(Poland).

- 'Władysław Anders', Wikipedia, http://en.wikipedia.org/wiki/W%C5%82adys%C5%82aw_Anders, accessed Oct. 2012.

Operation Tannenburg and Generalplan Ost:

- `Generalplan_Ost` http://www.worldfuturefund.org/wffmaster/Reading/GPO/gpoarticle.HTM

- `Generalplan_Ost` http://en.wikipedia.org/wiki/Generalplan_Ost accessed Dec. 2012

- `Holocaust Forgotten`, http://www.holocaustforgotten.com/poland.htm.

- `Holocaust: Non-Jewish Victims` http://www.holocaustforgotten.com/Newsletter.htm

- Jan Moor-Jankowski, `Poland's Holocaust` `Holocaust of Non-Jewish Poles during WWII`, http://www.warsawuprising.com/paper/jankowski1.htm http://www.pacwashmetrodiv.org/events/holoco4/moor-jankowski.htm.

- `Operation Tannenberg`, Wikipedia, http://en.wikipedia.org/wiki/Operation_Tannenberg, accessed Dec. 2012

- `Poles: Victims of the Nazi Era` http://www.ushmm.org/education/resource/poles/poles.php?menu=/export/home/www/doc_root/education/foreducators/include/menu.txt&bgcolor=CD9544

Polish Resettlement in England:

- `A Choice of Evils—Official British reaction to the Polish armed forces Question` http://www.angelfire.com/ok2/polisharmy/chapter2.html

- 'Army Units in Polish Resettlement Corps Camps in the UK 1946-1948', http://www.polishresettlementcampsintheuk.co.uk/PRC/PRC.htm.

- 'Polish Resettlement Camps in the UK 1946-1969' http://www.northwickparkpolishdpcamp.co.uk/.

- 'Polish Resettlement Corps', Wikipedia, http://en.wikipedia.org/wiki/Polish_Resettlement_Corps, accessed Oct. 2012.

- `Polish Second Corps` http://www.polandinexile.com/icrb.html

- `Polish Resettlement` http://www.polandinexile.com/polishresettlement.htm

- 'Resettlement Corps', Poland in Exile, www.polandinexile.com/polishresettlement.htm.

- Stoke & Staffordshire Polish Community http://www.bbc.co.uk/stoke/features/polish/polish_community.shtml

- *Polish in Scotland in the Second World war* http://www.makers.org.uk/place/PolishInScotland2WW

Betrayal of Poland:

- 'The French and British Betrayal of Poland in 1939', *World Future Fund*, http://www.worldfuturefund.org/wffmaster/reading/history/polandbetrayal.htm.

- 'Betrayal of Poland 1939-1945', *Patrick J. Buchanan: Official Website*, http://buchanan.org/blog/pjb-the-betrayal-of-poland-1939-1945-3.

Sources of Photographs

- 1, 2: United States Holocaust Memorial Museum, http://digitalassets.ushmm.org/photoarchives/ result.aspx?max_docs

- 3: War in Europe Begins, http://www.nww2m.com/2011/09/war-in-europe-begins/

- 4: Awesome Stories, http://www.awesomestories.com/assets/german-plane-over-warsaw

- 5, 6, 9: Battle of Tomaszow Lubelski, http://www.twcenter.net/forums/showthread.php?t=197146

- 8, 9, 63, 67, 68: Memories that Remain, http://cleopatra-memoriesthatremain.blogspot.co.uk /2010/09/Poland-tomaszow-lubelski-dziaania.html

- 10: Polish Vickers Mark E 6-ton tank, gallery, http://derela.republika.pl/en/vickersg

- 11, 32, 33, 36, 37: ARC Belzec, http://www.deathcamps.org/belzec/photos.html

- 12: Polish Site, http://www.polishsite.us/index.php/history-and-people/modern-history/395-solving-the-myth-polish-cavalry-charge-against-german-tanks.html

- 13: Battle of Bzura, http://ww2total.com/WW2/History/Chronology/1939/09/September-4-

- 14: Katiņas slaktiņš, http://lv.wikipedia.org/wiki/Kati%C5%86as_slakti%C5%86%C5%A1—

- 15: Les mrtvych v Katyne http://en.wikipedia.org/wiki/File:Les_mrtvych_v_Katyne.jpg

- 16: The History Place, http://www.historyplace.com/worldwar2/hitleryouth/

- 17, 19, 23: ARC Belzec Labour Camps, http://www.deathcamps.org/belzec/labourcamps

- 18: Jewish Cemetery of Tomaszow Mazowiecki, http://www.zchor.org/tomaszow/tpicture.

- 20, 21: Belzec Poland, http://www.jewishgen.org/forgottenCamps/Camps/BelzecEng.html

- 22: Dutch Tzedakah, http://www.dutchtzedakah.com/dt-ch12.htm

- 24: US Holocaust Museum, http://www.ushmm.org/wlc/en/media_ph.php?ModuleId

- 25: Death Camps Holocaust, https://deathcampsholocaust.wikispaces.com/Belzec+Death+

- 22 26, 27: Shoah: The Holocaust, http://www.zwoje-scrolls.com/shoah/towns.html

- 26: Untold Stories, http://www1.yadvashem.org/untoldstories/database/homepage.asp

- 28: Virtual Jerusalem, http://www.virtualjerusalem.com/judaism.php?Itemid=4923

- 29: Xtimeline History of the Holocaust, http://www.xtimeline.com/evt/view.aspx?id=18463

- 30: Spiegel International, http://www.spiegel.de/international/germany/bild-710866-50041.html

- 31: Holocaust Research Project, http://www.holocaustresearchproject.org/survivor/srebrnik.

- 34, 35: ARC Einsatzgruppen, http://www.deathcamps.org/occupation/einsatzgruppen.html

- 38 Expulsion of Polish Peasants in Zamasc http://en.wikipedia.org/wiki/Zamo%C5%9B%C4%87_Uprising

- 39, Zamosc Rotunda, http://www.cf2004.zamosc.pl/twierdza/rotunda_z_lotu_ptaka_en.htm

- 40: Wikimedia, http://upload.wikimedia.org/wikipedia/commons/6/6c/J%C4%99drusie_3

- 41: yadvashem, http://collections.yadvashem.org/photosarchive/en-us/19616.html

- 42, 43: Munich: The Camp Cosmos in a German Metropolis http://ausstellung-zwangsarbeit.org/en/286/

- 44: Władysław Anders, Wikipedia, http://en.wikipedia.org/wiki/WadyslawAnders

- 45: Odznaki Polskich, http://www.grawerapanasiuk.pl/PSZ_graf.htm

- 46: Surrounding Zone, http://www.valleluce.com/SurroundingZone.htm

- 47: WWII Behind Closed Doors, http://www.pbs.org/behindcloseddoors/in-depth/fighting

- 48: Poland in Exile, Polish 2nd Corp, http://www.polandinexile.com/icrb.html

- 49: Polish Force, http://www.ww2incolor.com/poland/p3.html

- 50: Polish Greatness, http://www.polishgreatness.com/montecassinophotogallery.html

- 51: The Hated Uniform Wojciech Zmyślony, http://www.wehrmacht-polacy.pl/w_psz.html& usg =ALkJrhg5rC9SPtHApRAovnhAAnqWewiS4A

- 52: Historia szkoly, http://www.spnr3tom.neostrada.pl/historia/historia.htm

- 53,54: Tomaszow Lubelski Photos, http://www.tomaszow.info/galeria/thumbnails.php?album

- 55: Epoch Times, http://www.theepochtimes.com/n2/opinion/polish-resolution-soviet-invasion-war-russia-22901.html

- 56: WH @KTHS World War II, http://dpeal.wikispaces.com/World+War+2

- 57: WWII Today, http://ww2today.com/soviet-troops-march-into-poland

- 58, 59, 60, 61, September Campaign, www.polishgreatness.com/septembercampaignphotogallery

- 62: WWII in Color, http:// http://www.ww2incolor.com/poland/1_046.html

- 64, 66: Stary Tomaszow Lubelski, http://www.maykelsc.neostrada.pl/www/stary/index1.html

- 65: Frontline Photos of German Soldiers, http://www.feldgrau.net/forum/viewtopic.php?

- Back Cover: First to Fight, Wikipedia, http://en.wikipedia.org/wiki/Polish_contribution_to_World_War_II

- Forest Landscape http://www.public-domain-image.com/cache/nature-landscapes-public-domain-images-pictures/forest-public-domain-images-pictures/snow-in-forest_w725_h544.jpg

- Poland—Public domain map http://www.worldofmaps.net/en/europe/map-poland/map-administrative-divisions-poland.htm

- Front Inside Cover:
Map of Poland:http://commons.wikimedia.org/wiki/File:EC_map_of_poland2.png#filehistory

Images of the Past

Tomaszow Lubelski during the 1930's—central market and churches.
(Photo sources 52, 53 and 54)

German troops (left) and Russian troops (right) marching into Poland.
(Photo sources 55, 56 and 57)

Polish cavalry, 1939. Russian excuse to invade. Russian planes over Poland.
(Photo sources 58, 59 and 60)

German and Russian Allies, 1939. Polish Infantry, 1939. Tomaszów-Zamosc Road, 1939.
(Photo sources 61, 62 and 63)

German tanks in Tomaszow, 1939. After the Battle of Tomaszow. Tomaszow after the War.
(Photo sources 64, 65 and 66)

The Author

Brendan Redko was born in Wolverhampton in 1955 and brought up in Bristol, England. After attending St Brendan's College, he left school in 1972 and went to St Luke's teacher training college in Exeter.

After qualifying as a teacher, he worked as a steel erector for three years before gaining employment at Whitefield Fishponds School and then Bristol Metropolitan Academy, one of the schools in the successful Cabot Learning Federation. He has worked there as a teacher of Physical Education for the last thirty-two years.

He lives with his partner, Ruth, and her son, Simon. He also has two children, Eddie and Kiri, and recently become a grandfather for the first time to Kiri's son, Zachary.

His biggest passion in life has always been sport, playing rugby to a good level before trying his skills at kick-boxing. He now spends most of his time coaching and organising school sports and activities as well as coaching and refereeing basketball in local leagues. His proudest achievement so far was winning a national award, The *Daily Telegraph* UK Sports Teacher of the Year, in 2006.

His active life now includes fire spinning, a performing art which involves spinning balls of fire on the end of chains around your body in a variety of patterns. He likes to perform this to music on beaches in the summer.

Brendan has always been a keen history student, and it was this interest which encouraged him to research this book. This is his first attempt at such a project, and he is particularly keen that it might provide a basic introduction and a few answers to anyone who wants to know a bit more about Polish history and maybe their own Polish ancestry.

Tomaszow Lubelski before and after the battle of Tomaszow in 1939.
(Photo sources 67, 68)

The Polish War Memorial in London.

Tomaszow Lubelski, 2011.